The Secret Art Of The Blowjob

Tips & Tricks To Please Him Every Time

by C.W. Pollard

Last year I wrote a book dedicated to the secret art of pussy eating (The Secret Art Of Eating Pussy: Tips & Tricks To Please Her Every Time ISBN 978-1463655631). It was well received. However, the release of that book has resulted in a number of communications asking me to provide a similarly written guide to those who are out there trying to please a man orally.

At first I thought it odd. Women asking a man to teach them to suck cock. It honestly seemed like a book that a woman should write. Then I thought about it. Most men have trouble openly discussing topics like this and have even more trouble explaining their ideas clearly and concisely. Often they are afraid of critiquing the blowjob performances of their lovers. They are often afraid of hurting their feelings. What I realized was happening was these women were asking for my help to make their sex lives more fulfilling and richer. Well, I am never one to shrink from a challenge. So, I sat down, thought a lot, and toiled a fair amount writing this little how to for all those out there looking to learn the secrets of a good blowjob.

I have also done an exhaustive empirical study into the subject of blowjobs from the point of view of both sexes. I'm not going to lie, I had to buy a lot of pitchers of beer and shots to get some of those girls and more of the guys to open up on the subject. However, they did. They shared many, many, juicy and intimate details about the subject. Also, my conversations have really run the gamut from man on man blowjobs, to woman on man blow jobs, to man and woman blowjobs...well, you get the point. I have hit all the bases.

So in essence, I have been the recipient and provider of a lot of oral sex and I have talked with my wide and varying peer group to get a true, intimate understanding of the blowjob from every perspective. The distillation of that essence is this work. It is my sincere hope, that through the study of this work, you will learn how to amaze, wow, tantalize and orally ravish the luck man in your life. Let's get started!

A Discussion Of Male Anatomy

In order to be able to successfully give a blowjob to a man, you need to have a basic understanding of a man's penis. When I wrote about eating pussy, I included a similar discussion. This is no different. However, a person interested in giving a blowjob does have one advantage over someone wanting to eat pussy. The vagina is a touch on the secretive side. Many of her secrets are hidden inside lips and folds of skin. With the penis, everything is very out in the open.

Obviously the penis itself is most prominent. However, I do want to highlight a few aspects of the penis that will be helpful to you in your quest to master the art of the blowjob. The penis is actually made up of several parts and they differ in sensitivity and how you stimulate them.

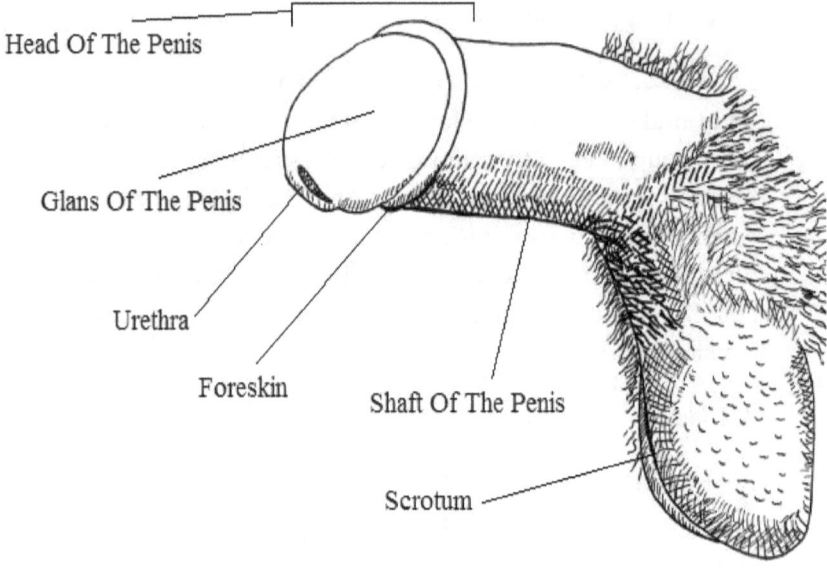

Head Of The Penis

Glans Of The Penis

Urethra

Foreskin

Shaft Of The Penis

Scrotum

At the very tip of the penis, you will find the opening of the man's urethra. This is where he will ejaculate from. This opening is at the very center of what is often called the glans of the penis. The man is most sensitive at this point. The highest concentration of nerves on the penis are found here. This means this is where you can stimulate him the most. As you move out from the opening of his urethra along the skin of the "helmet" of his penis, this concentration of nerves decreases rapidly. By the time you reach the shaft of his penis, the sensitivity has fallen sharply. When you are stimulating a penis with your mouth, you really only need to focus on the "helmet" of his penis for this reason. This is the most pleasure sensitive area of his whole body.

As a way to help put everything in context, I want to remind the reader about a fact of biology. When a human embryo is just beginning to develop, male and female embryos are essentially identical. If everything continues on uninterrupted, the embryo will develop female. However, if the right hormones are in place, the embryo will undergo a few modifications and turn male. In this process, the tissues that would normally form the clitoris elongates and develops and turns into a penis. The tissue that would form vaginal lips instead seal up and form his scrotum. That's why that seam runs up the middle of it.

Think of it this way and you will do very well. The same nerves that are present in your clitoris are the same nerves that are present in the glans of your lover's penis. The way you like your clitoris to be stimulated orally, is the same way that he wants his penis to be stimulated by your mouth.

I do want to pause for a moment and discuss foreskin. If your partner is not circumcised, it will be necessary for you to wrap your fingers around his penis and slowly push down towards his balls to reveal the tip of his penis. It is entirely possible that the entire tip of his penis is concealed by the foreskin when his penis is limp. This is where the term "snake in a sweater" comes from. If this is the case, do not be alarmed. Once he becomes hard and you apply the pressure to the foreskin I described above, the tip of his penis will be revealed and everything else is the same.

Continuing down the male anatomy, we next come to the shaft of the penis. This area is considerably less sensitive than the glans of his penis. Your mouth can be used in this area for playful licking and kissing, or even deep throating. However, it is not required here in order to give a good blowjob.

Below the shaft of the penis we come to the man's testicles. Now, here women are often stumped. I honestly can't blame them. The testicles and the scrotum are a bit of a mystery. Women know that men like attention here, however, they are often afraid of causing any harm. OK, here is the guiding principle surrounding the testicles. Just be gentle. Yes, men like attention to their balls. The enjoy it. However, you need to be gentle. You can kiss, lick, lightly suck or lightly caress. Support is good too. Cup them and hold them with your free hand. However, remember that roughly sucking or grabbing can quickly ruin the party. If you are ever unsure, start very, very gently and work your way up slowly. You will find the right attention for the man you are playing with quickly enough.

Below his balls you will find his perenium. This is often called the "taint". This particular area is not terribly sensitive, however, you can definitely give it some attention. If you don't want to go here, don't worry. You will can still give him an amazingly wonderful blowjob without ever paying this area any attention.

Lastly, we come to his anus. It is true that some men like to have their anus played with during a blowjob. It can be kissed, licked or even fingered. However, many women are uncomfortable with this. If you are, don't give it a second thought. What I said about the "taint" is just as true here. However, if you are one of those people who really wants to play with an anus (I can be one of them from time to time to), you need to leave it alone until you have talked with your partner. This is one of those areas where communication is key. You need to talk and see what they think. A surprise anus raid is never something that should happen. Both partners need to be into it and excited by it, or it shouldn't happen.

Now that we are on the same page concerning the important points of a man's anatomy, we can get down to our technical discussion of blowjobs. Let's move on.

Communication Is Still Key

I stressed this in my book on pussy eating and I want to stress this again in this work. The best way to achieve a successful environment for passionate, erotic, hot, mind blowing oral sex is through communication. I can and will teach you a lot of techniques in this book, however, only through communication can you learn how your particular partner likes them to be applied.

You need to be able to talk to him, and you need to talk to him about your blowjobs. Now, don't go and take any criticism as meaning you are a poor cock sucker. On the contrary! The fact that you know that every man is different and that only through talking to him can you learn how to blow him perfectly, already makes you a better blowjobber than most of the women out there.

I would recommend three ways that you can communicate about his enjoyment and your technique. If you are normally shy, don't be. Every man loves talking about blowjobs.

First, you can do a pregame conversation. This is when you ask what he likes before you have his throbbing member staring you in the face. Ask him what was the best blowjob he ever had. Ask him what he likes to have done. This alone will be more than enough to start getting blood flowing to his crotch. You can gain a lot of insight about his particular pleasure triggers from this conversation.

The next opportunity to engage in communication is during the blowjob itself. Now, in this situation, you are not going to be able to carry on an extensive deep dialog.

If you are talking a a lot during a blowjob, I'm sorry, but you're doing it wrong. Limit yourself to the simple question; "Do you like that?". Look him in the eye when you say it and see how he reacts. Is he excited and enthusiastic? If he is, you are on the right track. Now, don't go and ask this every two seconds. That will make him feel like you are interrogating him. Limit yourself to asking this question three times. Other than that, you will need to rely on his body movements to see if he is enjoying what you are doing. We will talk about that more later.

The last opportunity you will have to talk to your man about your blowjob performance is after the blowjob is over. The best time is while he is basking in the afterglow and is still a little drunk from the orgasm you just gave him with your mouth. Ask him if he liked it. Ask him what his favorite part was. Most likely his answers will be short and to the point, but they will be honest.

The Basic Blowjob Technique

When I wrote "The Secret Art Of Eating Pussy: Tips & Tricks To Please Her Every Time", I advised the reader of that book to forget about all the bells and whistles and simply focus on stimulating the clitoris in a basic manner. All to often in our lives we seek to complicate the simple and in doing so lose sight of our goal. The same is true with blowjobs.

The primary goal of the blowjob is simply to use your mouth to make the man orgasm. That's it. To do that, all you need to do is to stimulate the glans of his penis with your mouth, while at the same time, stimulating the shaft of the penis with your hand. That's it! Congratulations, you just learned the first secret to giving really good head. Keep that simple goal in mind and the men in your life will think you are amazing at giving oral sex in no time.

Now, there are some details to work out to give this basic blowjob. First, you need to focus on body positioning. You can really suck a cock in more ways than I could possibly describe. You can come at it from an almost infinite number of ways. However, just like there is a basic pussy eating position, there is a basic blow job position as well.

The easiest way to give a basic blowjob is to have your lover lie down on the bed. You can have them stand, but honestly, he can stumble when he's cumming and your knees can get sore. A bed fixes both of these problems. Have him spread his legs and you get between them facing him. This position is also good, because when you put his penis in your mouth, your tongue will be along the bottom of his glans. This will increase stimulation.

You should be up on your knees. You are going to be using your hands here, so you cannot rely on them to support your body. You arms should be able to have full freedom of motion. That being said, take hold of his penis with your hand (for brevity, I am assuming he's already erect). Your hand should be holding his penis like you would a bottle of beer. Your thumb should be on the same side that you are and the outside of your pinky should be resting on his body, just where his penis attaches.

Now, you are going to stroke his penis with your hand. Don't worry, we're going to get your mouth involved, but we have to build to that. Gently grasp his penis and move your hand up it. When he is hard, you will feel the skin slide over the muscle in his penis. This is perfect. Gently, at first, slide your hand up the shaft of the penis until the edge of your index finger touches the start of the helmet of his penis. Once you have hit that point, do the opposite and slide your hand back down until your pinky touches his body. This is the basic blowjob hand motion.

Now, you will notice that the basic blowjob hand motion does nothing for the tip of his penis. You may be wondering why this is, since we have already talked about how many nerves are there and how stimulated that little patch of skin can get. Well, have no fear, that is where your mouth comes in.

Go ahead and place the tip of his penis in your mouth. All you really need in there is the helmet of the penis. That is really all that is necessary for giving a good, basic blowjob. Hold in in your mouth and slowly slide your tongue from side to side on the underside of the tip of his cock. Suck in ever so slightly to create just the faintest hint of pressure. You do not need to compete with the vacuum cleaner. Think gentle pressure only. This is the basic blowjob mouth motion.

The goal of the basic blowjob is to combine the basic blowjob hand motion with the basic blowjob mouth motion. The two together make the overall experience so much more pleasurable than either one could ever be on it own. Go ahead and try it at this point if you can. Now, don't start to fast with your hand or you will be hitting yourself in the face. Start slowly and get the rhythm down. It won't take long. Actually, starting slow in the beginning will help to heighten his arousal. Speed up when you are more comfortable and really go to town when he shouts out "I'm going to cum. Don't Stop!".

Congratulations. You have just learned how to perform a basic blowjob. That forms the core of this book. Everything else that we will discuss adds to and enhances this concept. However, trust me, with this information alone, you are perfectly capable of pleasing any man in your life.

Lube, Lube, Lube

When you are stroking the shaft of his penis at the same time that you have the tip in your mouth, you are going to be applying some friction. This is good. This is what is stimulating him and what will ultimately lead to his orgasm. However, just like friction in your vagina, lubrication helps to make everything work smoothly and pleasurably.

Now, I am not telling you to squirt a water based lube all over his junk. This will just cause a sticky mess and wind up in your mouth. You don't need or want this to occur. Instead, rely on your saliva to keep everything lubricated.

What you need to do is literally drool on his cock as you are sucking it. Don't worry one second that he will be upset that you are drooling all over his cock. In fact, he will probably really get off on it. Some of the best blowjobs I have ever had are the sloppiest, drooliest ones. The saliva keeps everything lubricated until I am orgamsing.

As a twist to the whole drooling on his cock concept while you are sucking and stroking it, you can always spit on his dick to keep it lubed. Spitting on it has the same lubricating effect that discreetly drooling on it does with one added advantage. He will see it and hear it. The act of spitting on his cock will appeal very much to almost any man out there. Think of it as a showwoman's way of keeping everything good and wet. You achieve a necessary function at the same time you heighten his arousal. Whatever you choose to do, just keep his cock well lubricated while you are stroking it.

Don't Stop Until Your Told To

One of the worst things that any woman can do while giving a blowjob is to stop prematurely. This can have disastrous results. Imagine the last time that you got oral sex and had an orgasm. You might be smiling with reminiscences. Well, now try and imagine your lover stopping right at that critical moment that your orgasm was peaking. Boom! All of a sudden all of the stimulation is gone. That wonderful orgasm that had been building for what seemed like forever vanishes. Worst of all, at that point, there is no way to get it back. You've missed it like a bus on a rainy day and you're stuck out in the cold. Now you've got sexual frustration instead of orgasmic afterglow.

Well, men and women are not really that different and our orgasms are based on similar processes in our bodies. When he begins to ejaculate his orgasm is only just beginning to peak. Trust me, the first drop of semen does not mean his orgasm is over. It is only starting. What he needs to truly climax at that moment is the same consistent stimulation that you have applied up to this point. Stopping prematurely, when you feel the first spurt of semen, will just ruin his orgasm.

This means two things. First, it means that you are going to have to deal with his semen one way or another. I will talk about the options that you have at your disposal later on. However, you need to plan this out before your mouth starts filling with semen. Next, it means that in order to truly give a fantastic, amazing blowjob, you are going to need to continue your mouth work until he has finished his orgasm. Just as your clitoris becomes super sensitive after orgasm, the tip of his penis will too. At a certain point it is so sensitive that he will not be able to tolerate your sucking and will tell you to stop. Either that, or his cock will begin to go limp. Those are the two signs that you have that it is safe to stop. Either he will tell you or his cock will. Either way, wait til then.

Cumming In The Mouth...Let's Talk

A lot of women out there are intimidated by the thought of having their lover cum in their mouths. As such, they do one of two things.

The first thing that often occurs when a woman is afraid of getting some semen in her mouth, is that she just flat out refuses to give her lover oral sex. Now, of course this is her prerogative, however, in doing so she is denying her lover a pleasurable and very intimate form of sex and she is missing out on all the positive rewards of performing a blowjob. Performing a blowjob successfully makes you feel attractive, sexy, appreciated and the pure act of giving pleasure to your lover is pleasurable to you. Obviously, missing out on all this is not good.

The other thing that a woman with a semen phobia is going to do is give a half assed blowjob and stop the oral stimulation about halfway through. Then she will usually manually stimulate her lover until he cums all over her. She is fine with this, she just doesn't want to get it in her mouth. This can be fine, but honestly, it is going to be a pretty unimpressive blowjob.

He wants to cum in your mouth. There, I said it. You just need to accept it. If you are going to become a blowjob goddess, which is the aim of this book, you are just going to have to come to grips with the fact that you are going to need to let your lover cum in your mouth. It may be awkward at first. So is eating oysters, however, you will get used to it and probably, in the long run learn to enjoy it.

Let me explain why he wants to cum in your mouth in a manner that you can most likely relate to. I am going to assume that you, as a woman, have received oral sex before and orgasm ed from it. Close your eyes and imagine the warm wet sensation of your lovers mouth all over your pussy. It feels great. You are starting to build towards orgasm and you can feel all those little tremors in your thighs starting to shoot off. You can't want. You get closer and closer as the person between your thighs pleasures you in perfect rhythm with your own movements. Then...they stop and start trying to give you an orgasm with just their fingers. The magic will get broken. You may be able to get there eventually, but now, everything is different. You are a little frustrated and you have to start all over.

That scenario is exactly what is happening when you take his penis out of your mouth and switch to giving him a handjob. He may get there eventually, but usually it will be frustrating and the magic is gone.

Instead, just plan on letting him cum in your mouth. You don't have to swallow anything and I will give you several techniques to deal with the semen.

Overcoming The Fear Of Ejaculation

The first point that needs to be addressed before you are comfortable dealing with semen in your mouth is we need to get you over the fear of him cumming in your mouth. A lot of women are afraid of this. There is nothing wrong with that fear. It is a little odd and the act is foreign. Of course they have all heard horror stories from their friends about choking and what not. No one likes water going down their throat when they are swimming and semen in your throat is pretty much the same thing.

As a rule, when he is about to cum, you should just have the tip of his penis in your mouth. This will help you to control the ejaculation and it will also reduce the chance of any semen going down your windpipe. This is to be avoided, as it will prompt a violent coughing fit.

It is not at all unreasonable to ask your lover to tell you when they are getting close to orgasm. This opens the channels of communication and serve three very good purposes. The first purpose is that you will not be caught with a mouthful of semen while you are unprepared. You can get ready for it and deal with it accordingly when it happens. Secondly, just like when someone is eating your pussy, you don't want things to change when he is very close to orgasm anyway. Calling out that he is about to cum will help you keep the rhythm steady and ensure that his orgasm occurs without any frustrating interruptions. The last purpose that this serves is to build trust between a couple. You will be able to trust that he is not going to cum in your mouth without telling you. This will help you relax and really begin to enjoy giving him pleasure and feeling sexy and empowered in return.

Before you begin to give him a blowjob, ask him to tell you when he is about to cum. Trust me, he will be more than happy to accommodate your request if it means he gets a blowjob and gets to cum in your mouth.

You should know that when a man is ejaculating the head of his penis is going to swell quite a bit in your mouth. This is going to be perceptible right before he cums. This is a physical tip from his body to get ready. You should be waiting and looking for this tip. When you feel that, you know that he is about to ejaculate and again you can make sure only the tip is in your mouth. At this point keep up your hand motion and you will ensure a perfectly controlled release into your mouth.

Now, as for your mouth itself, with only the tip of his penis in your mouth (no deep throating at this point) you are really in control of how he ejaculates. What you can do is tilt your forehead down as you angle the opening of his penis directly onto your tongue. You can even cup your tongue to receive the semen. This will form a perfect receptacle for the semen to collect and will make sure that none winds up in your throat, at the same time the blowjob completes in a smooth, natural finish.

Now all you need to do is figure out what to do with that semen.

What To Do With That Semen

Well, the old adage of spit or swallow really illustrates the two choices that you face when a man is cumming in your mouth. Those are your two options really. However, I do have a few words to add to the discussion.

First, if you really just can't stand semen in your mouth, one thing you can do is this. When you have angled your forehead down and he is cumming onto your tongue, you can open your mouth. What will happen at this point, is that as the semen is released, it will run right down your tongue onto his balls. This is the fastest way to get it out of your mouth. Also, you won't have to stop any oral pleasuring to do this.

If this is to much coordination, you can hold the semen in your mouth and then elegantly spit it into a towel that you cleverly placed next to the bed. If you think you can't hold semen in your mouth, you are wrong. Just go gargle some water and you will realize how much you are in control of swallowing after all.

If you do decide to swallow, it is really not bad. I have tasted semen plenty of times and the flavor is really quite benign. If you do decide to swallow just do it quickly and I would recommend a quick swig of water as well. You should always have water and a towel next to the bed whenever there is wild oral sex going on. It's just best to be prepared.

So those are your options as far as semen in the mouth is concerned.

If You Really Just Can't Do Semen In The Mouth

Some people just cannot deal with semen in their mouth. They just can't. Well if this is the case, it is much better to use one of these tricks I am about to show you than it is to vomit or have a panic attack. Trust me, these are better.

The first trick is to use a blowjob as just foreplay. This is when you use your mouth to simply get him excited enough to engage in intercourse. He can then orgasm inside of you and the whole issue of semen in the mouth is sidestepped. This is really a great tip. Like I've said, a blowjob without orgasm as a means of foreplay is a great way to get him excited and often cumming inside someone during intercourse is just as good if not better than cumming in their mouth. It's the old bait and switch and he and his cock will never complain. Trust me.

The next option you have is to manually stroke his penis with your hand until he orgasms. The way I see it, if you choose this technique, you have two options. The first is that you have him cum on you. Many men find this very arousing. I am not one to cum on a woman's face. Honestly I have never gotten the appeal of that, but many men like this. Cumming on a woman's breasts are also very popular. There is an element of domination and territory marking here that definitely appeals to a man's mind (even on a subconscious level).

If you really can't deal with semen in your mouth, just follow one of the these moves listed in this section and you should be just fine. Remember, you can also always work your way up to semen in the mouth. This has been the case for me with women in my life, and often their attitudes change over time. Just do what works for you.

Oral Sex Foreplay

At this point, I have discussed in detail the basic blowjob. You should think of the basic blowjob as the technique that you use when it is time to make a man orgasm. This should not take long. A well rythmed basic blowjob should have little trouble making a man cum in less than five minutes or so. In some cases, this is exactly what you want. However, I would strongly encourage you, as you work to become an expert on oral sex, to take your time with a blowjob. Although there is work involved, it should not be a chore. Instead, it should be play between two concerning adults who care for each other. It should be fun. There should be teasing. There should be slow licking and gentle kissing. You should work up to the basic blowjob slowly. Don't rush. There should be as much foreplay to an act of oral sex as there is to an act of intercourse. If you just get in there and bang it out, you are missing out on so much of the magic, fun and passion.

I am not going to give you a play by play method for foreplay. That would defeat the whole point. All that I will say is that you should work to give slow, soft attention to every part of his bikini zone. Only when you feel he is good and relaxed and at the same time thoroughly aroused, then should you start to actually stimulate him to orgasm with the basic blowjob technique.

Deep Throating

So much is made of deep throating these days. The adult film industry and popular culture make this sexual act out to be the greatest thing in the oral sex realm. Well, let me tell you, it's all crap. You most definitely do not need to be able to deep throat to give an amazing blowjob.

Actually, since we know that the vast majority of a penis' nerves are at the very tip, you know that you don't stimulate anything extra by shoving the whole thing down your throat. Sure, it is a nice trick if you can do it, however, it is not at all necessary. The steps listed in the basic blowjob section are all that is required. So, if you gag, or are intimidated by deep throating, don't give it a second thought. Stick to the basics and master those. I'm confident the men in your life will not even notice because you will already be an amazing cocksucker. Trust me.

You Can Get Good & Rough

One thing that I want to make clear to all you ladies is that the penis is tough. It is really designed to be a battering ram. A lot of women seem to be very cautious about hurting a man's cock. They look at a penis through the lens of their pussies, which by comparison, are delicate and sensitive. Don't worry. You can spank, bite, nibble, pinch and vigorously stroke his cock all you want.

Now, there is one area that you need to be delicate with and that is his balls. These are sensitive and can be harmed if you are not careful. We will talk more about his balls and just what you are supposed to do with them in a bit.

Eye Contact

A lot of women do not understand the effect and connection that can be created when you make eye contact during a blowjob. Again, this is simply a result of the differences between men and women. Women, when they are getting their pussies eaten, tend to focus on the physical sensation. They do not watch the man (or woman) between their thighs intently. For them, the show is secondary. This is definitely not the case for men.

Men very much want to watch you suck their cocks. They will be watching you intently and they will be enjoying what they see. You can add to that with eye contact. Looking him intently in the eyes while he watches his cock slide into your mouth will only heighten his pleasure. It will say that you are turned on by what you are doing and that his pleasure is important to you. A woman looking into the eyes of the man who she is blowing is not a woman who is doing him a favor, but is a woman very much enjoying the sexual act she is performing. This is incredibly arousing to men.

Eye contact also has the effect of creating connection between the couple. By looking him in the face, you will be able to see his reactions of pleasure. This is a great way to learn through direct observation what he enjoys.

Non-Goal Oriented Blowjobs

When I described the basic blowjob in an earlier part of this work, I was outlining a series of steps that are guaranteed to make the man in your life cum, and cum quickly, through your oral loving. The entire process should not take more than a few minutes of vigorous suck/stroking. This might be perfect for those quickie blowjobs when you duck into the ladies room at a concert or off the trail on a hike. However, if that were all that I taught you, I would be doing you quite a disservice.

There is a lot more to blowjobs than just a basic quickie. Men and women share a love of attention and the thought of their lover's hands, mouth and body. Ask yourself a question. When a partner of yours is eating your pussy, do you want them to charge right for your clitoris and begin vigorously stimulating it? I will assume you said no. Well, men are no different. That's where non-goal oriented oral sex comes in. If the basic blowjob provides you with the fundamentals of fellatio skills, this concept is where you add the passion, playfulness and fun.

There is not a step by step playbook for this part of oral sex. What unfolds between two lovers in the middle of this act is deeply personal and will be driven by their collective souls, spirits, hearts and passions. I can't tell you what to do. However, I can tell you how to know what to do.

Imagine having your lover lie on the bed again like when I told you how to give the basic blowjob. His head is at the top of the bed and you are facing him at the foot. Imagine that you trade places. How would you want your lover to touch you? Where would you like them to kiss, lick, suck nibble or caress? How would you like them to touch you?

Where would you like attention? What would you like them to whisper in your ear? How would you want them to look at you while the kissed your most intimate and sensitive places? This is how you should touch him. Take your time. Explore his body and savor his reactions to your touch and kiss. Take your time. His excitement and arousal will only build. As a good measure of his arousal, look for the tell tale signs of pre-cum at the tip of his penis.

Two bits of advice that I will offer you however, are to always pay attention to his cock. No matter how the two of you contort your bodies, you should somehow always be paying attention to his penis. Men tend to be more impatient than women, and can frustrate. However, if you are always paying attention to his cock, this shouldn't happen. He will be wondering what you are going to do next. Also, don't be afraid to tell him your intentions. Whispering "I'm going to make you cum in my mouth." will most certainly communicate your intentions to pleasure him orally in no uncertain terms. Men will appreciate the directness, even if you take your time in getting there.

The Blowjob As Foreplay

Where a woman is concerned, you cannot stop eating her pussy and switch to intercourse only for her to cum moments later. It just doesn't work that way. However, the same is not true at all with the blowjob. You can suck your man until he is moments away from cumming, stop, and slip it inside you only for him to happily pump himself to orgasm and fuck you silly in the process. In fact, this is often a lot of fun.

What I am really saying here is that blowjobs are not simply a suck him until he cums or don't put your mouth anywhere near his cock problem. There is a wide range of possibilities here and you and he will have a lot of fun exploring them. Blowjobs can most definitely be a very, very fun bit of foreplay. You would be silly to ignore that facet of the blowjob in your sex life.

Spirit Of 69

Men are much more visually oriented than women and focus a great deal on what they see to turn them on. Knowing this, you should not be surprised that men are big fans of the "69" position. You can most definitely incorporate this into your oral sex games.

To do this, you should have your gentleman friend lie on the bed. Have his head about two feet from the top. If this means his legs dangle off the end of the bed, so be it. Now, straddle his face so you are looking at his feet. Once you have done this, you can then place his penis in his mouth and begin your blowjob.

If you choose to play with 69, there are a few things that you should know. First, most women are going to have trouble orgasming from anything he is going to be doing down there. The coordination required to keep the blowjob going is going to distract most women. Also, the body positioning of the 69 is really just not good for pussy eating. He is coming at her clitoris the wrong way to properly stimulate it. If you do 69, you should really just consider it adding another element (i.e. Your pussy right in his face) to the blowjob. This is still about his pleasure at this point. Of course, his mouth on your pussy may be more than enough to get you wet and constitutes a very good bit of foreplay.

If you choose to blow him to orgasm in the 69 position, you are also going to need to rethink your mouth positioning when he orgasms. It is still possible to direct the ejaculation onto your tongue, but you are going to need to stretch your neck a bit. Also, you may not be able to hear him call out before he orgasms. He may be muffled by your thighs and pussy. That's OK too. Generally as he approaches orgasm, he will stop licking your pussy. He will be too distracted. Take this as your cue.

The Quickie Blowjob

Like I have said, the basic blow job technique that was outlined earlier in this work, should be more than capable of bringing a man to orgasm in just a few short minutes. Start to finish. A man can also be ready willing and able for oral sex in just a few minutes. With the design of male attire he can also have his penis out in no time. These three facts make possible the quickie blowjob.

The quickie blowjob is when a couple decides to engage in oral sex while out and about. This can happen any number of places. Maybe they duck into an elevator or a public restroom together. Perhaps a deserted stairwell. Maybe on a hiking trail.

This can be a fun, naughty way for two people to engage in sex that can add a lot of excitement to a relationship. This is generally considerably more possible than eating a woman's pussy on the go (although it can be done) and is something that you should discuss with your lover. For many, the thrill of getting caught only adds to the fun!

Practice Makes Perfect

A while ago, a woman and I were sitting in a restaurant having lunch. She is a friend of mine and we were having a lively conversation. We talked about our lives and what we were up to and what was going on. Well, of course, I discussed this project with her. There are no secrets between the two of us. She laughed, and like most women when I told them about this work, started volunteering tips, tricks and advice. A lot of it wasn't new. However, she did tell me a pretty amusing story that I think is relevant to our discussion.

Apparently, she did not lose her virginity until she was 19. Until that time she had been a bit prudish. Like so many young women, her freshman year at college had been a bit of a turning point. She told me that she needed to learn how to give a blowjob and was simply mortified at the idea of seeming inexperienced (which she was) when the time came for her to get to work.

Well, she came up with a plan. She went out and bought herself a realistic dildo (veins and everything) and her and her roommate spent a fair amount of time getting comfortable with a cock shaped object in their mouths. She said she even learned to deep throat with it!

Now, for me, this sort of thing had been akin to the slumber party sleepover pillow fight. I had just assumed that it was a figment of our collective imaginations. To find myself face to face with a woman who was confirming that college coeds stay up late learning to give blowjobs together was more than appealing. However, I realized that she had brought up an, until then, ignored point.

If you want to get good at something and not seem inexperienced (a common enough fear for all of us), you need to practice. Why would blowjobs be any different? Why would we expect perfection right out of the gate?

You can find this experience in only one of two ways. Find a partner who is not going to mind working up your cock sucking expertise, or you can find a cock shaped object and practice on your own. If you don't feel comfortable buying a realistic dildo (although you can do this virtually anonymously on the internet), try the vegetable section of your local grocery store. I'm thinking carrot.

You Are In Control – Enjoy It

One thing that anyone planning to suck a cock should understand, is that they are most definitely in control. When you have a man's cock in your mouth, he is completely at your mercy. You control whether or not he will be happy or sad, and whether or not he will receive the one thing he wants most in the world – to orgasm in your mouth. Everything else fades into the background. He would do anything, say anything to please you to finish. You may be on your knees, but you are the one in charge. Often, you can use this to heighten the blowjob and your sense of control. Feel free to tease him. Keep him guessing as to your intentions. He is putty i your hands here, if nowhere else. You can and should enjoy the control as much as you do the pleasure you are giving him.

"It Turns Me On When You Tell Me What To Do"

A lot of men have trouble discussing what they like during sex. They are happy to stick it in, move it around a bit until they cum. However, that doesn't tell you anything about what turns them on and what they enjoy from you and doing to you. This is a huge roadblock to giving a good blowjob. You are going to need to get them to talk to you and tell them what they like.

The best way to do that is to use a little psychology. Men want their women to be turned on by them. This is important to them. They want you to enjoy sex. So what you do is this. You tell them that you are going to give them a blowjob, and you want them to tell you what to do. You tell them that they are the boss and it turns you on for them to boss you around. Most men will only be too happy to oblige. In bossing you around, they are really telling you what they enjoy and they are having you do it. In all reality, they are giving you a one on one class on how to give them a tailor made, perfect blowjob.

Dealing With A Limp Cock

In my sex life I have dealt with a limp cock plenty of times. You need to not be intimidated by this. It is entirely possible that you are getting hot in heavy in the back of a car in the parking lot of some mall, you pull down his pants with the intention of taking the head of his hard cock in your mouth, only to find that things are not especially hard down there. To some women, this is going to be a huge ego hit and they may not recover from it.

This doesn't need to be the case. A limp cock is by no means an insult or a sign that the man is not into what is happening. When you first start making out, does your pussy immediately become wet? No, this can take time and direct stimulation. Well a penis is no different. It just needs a little direct attention and it will be rock hard in no time. Actually, with a penis, it's very easy. Just take the whole limp thing and put it in your mouth. Play with it with your tongue while you gently cup his balls and it will be hard in no time. In fact, you will actually feel it getting hard in your mouth as you do this. In no time, he will have a full fledged erection that will be already lubed with your saliva and you can commence the wonderful blowjob you had planned on.

The Don't Call It A BlowJOB For Nothing

Anyone who cares about the pleasure of their partner enough to engage in oral sex, needs to be able to come to grips with the fact there may be some discomfort. Let's just put it on the table and talk about it. When I am eating a woman's pussy this is definitely the case. My neck can get stiff, my wrist may get tired, my jaw can get sore. Maybe I'm under the covers and its getting pretty hot and sweaty down there. Why should it be any different when I give a blowjob?

In my conversations with the ladies in my life concerning the act of sucking a man's cock, they have reported many of the same occurrences. Their jaws and wrists get tired and their necks get sore. So what? When you run a marathon, you know you are going to be sore when you're done. However, it feels absolutely wonderful when you finish. Well, the same is true for oral sex. Sure there may be some (mild at worst) discomfort along the way, but in the end, that all means nothing when you feel your lovers body tense in pleasure and relax at release. You feel great at the pure act of giving them pleasure and the sense of accomplishment. So when you're in there, on your knees, cock in your mouth and you start feeling those muscles beginning to ache, ignore it. Focus on your lover and their pleasure. In the end, you will find it worthwhile.

Sometimes It Just Ain't Gonna Happen...It's OK

 I said this in my work on pussy eating and I would by a bit of a hypocrite if I did not include the same message in this work. So here goes. Sometimes you can suck his cock all you want and do it perfectly, just to have him not reach orgasm. It's OK. Don't beat yourself up. Orgasms and human sexuality can be a little tricky. This is art, not science. Remember that.

Lot's of things can cause this. Maybe his head isn't in the right place. Maybe he had a rough day at work. Maybe you came home horny, just after he had masturbated (been there done that) and he just won't fess up. No matter how good that blowjob is, you're not going to make him cum two minutes later.

You can't go through life expecting everything to be perfect. It definitely should not be read that you did something wrong, he doesn't find you attractive, or that you should give up on oral sex as a whole. That would just be silly. Instead, talk about it. Put it out on the open and reassure each other about your feelings. Be patient and understanding That is the healthy adult thing to do. That and try giving him a blowjob tomorrow just for good measure. I very much doubt he will argue with you.

What's Good For The Goose

I am a big believer in equality. Equality in a relationship along with a give and take spirit of compromise is one of the keys to a long lasting, supportive, mutually beneficial, and healthy relationship. That concept applies to the bedroom as much as it does to any facet of your relationship. If you are reading this book, you are interested in pleasing your lover. It is as pleasurable to me to give oral sex as it is to receive it. However, I sure as hell like to get it. If you are going to all this trouble to learn to please your lover, it is my sincere hope that they are just as interested in pleasing you orally.

After reading this book, I am sure that you will be excited to go out and try all that I have taught you. At the same time, I hope that you will insist, if need be, on your lover getting down on their knees and pleasuring you as well. Never forget what's good for the goose is good for the gander.

In Conclusion

Thank you for reading this work. At this point, I am hopeful that you have learned much about how to pleasure a man orally. We have covered lots of techniques, tips and tricks in our little discussion. Now, it is up to you to put this all together and become a true blowjob goddess. I am sincerely hopeful that you will be able to do this. Always remember to enjoy yourself and to have fun. Also remember to keep the communication open and flowing. A blowjob is just like another sexual act. It is a partnership and requires the two of you to operate in harmony. Good luck and enjoy!

-C.W. Pollard